W9-BVH-047

WHAT'S DARWIN Got to Do WITH It?

A Friendly Conversation About Evolution

Robert C. Newman & John L. Wiester
with Janet & Jonathan Moneymaker

InterVarsity Press
Downers Grove, Illinois

InterVarsity Press
P.O. Box 1400, Downers Grove, IL 60515
World Wide Web: www.ivpress.com
E-mail: mail@ivpress.com

InterVarsity Press® is the book-publishing division of InterVarsity Christian Fellowship/USA®, a student movement active on campus at hundreds of universities, colleges and schools of nursing in the United States of America, and a member movement of the International Fellowship of Evangelical Students. For information about local and regional activities, write Public Relations Dept., InterVarsity Christian Fellowship/USA, 6400 Schroeder Rd., P.O. Box 7895, Madison, WI 53707-7895.

ISBN 0-8308-2249-6

Printed in the United States of America ∞

Library of Congress Cataloging-in-Publication Data

What's Darwin got to do with it: a friendly conversation about evolution / Robert C. Newman . . . [et al.].
    p. cm.
  Includes bibliographical references.
  ISBN 0-8308-2249-6 (pbk. : alk. paper)
    1. Evolution (Biology) 2. Creationism. I. Newman, Robert C. (Robert Chapman),
1941-

QH367.W57 2000
576.8—dc21

                                                 99-055902

16   15   14   13   12   11   10   9   8   7   6   5   4   3   2

12   11   10   09   08   07   06   05   04   03   02   01   00

Contents

99530

We are grateful to the Discovery Institute's Center for the Renewal of Science and Culture for its technical, critical and financial support and to IBRI for its financial assistance over the course of this project

Preface

"Where do we come from?"

"Why are we here?"

In our culture we find dramatically different answers to these questions. Some say we are made in the image of God, who designed us for a purpose and wants us to experience life to the full. Others say we are we byproducts of an impersonal and mindless process that cares nothing for us. Who is right? And how should we then live? Should we treat one another as persons or mere machines?

How we answer these questions has a lot to do with which creation story we believe. The power to tell us where we come from is the power to tell us who we are and how we ought to live.

There are two major creation stories in our culture. One story is theistic. It asserts that a preexisting intelligence created and designed the universe, life and human beings.

The other story is a materialistic one. It asserts that only matter-energy has always existed and that life owes its origin to a process of undirected evolutionary change from molecules to humanity.

Though both creation stories have profound implications for how we live, the materialistic story has become the official creation story for our culture. It is the only story taught in our public schools. Many biology texts teach it as a fact, whereas the other story, when mentioned, is treated as merely a subjective belief. The materialistic story has preserved its monopoly status because many have assumed that all available scientific evidence supports it. On the other hand, many have rejected the theistic story because they assume that science has failed to find evidence for intelligent design. This book will take a critical look at those assumptions.

What's Darwin got to do with it? The materialistic creation story has derived its main support from a theory known as Darwinism. The principal claim of Darwin's theory was that the mechanism of natural selection explains how enormously complex life forms could arise without the aid of an intelligent designer. In the words of Francisco Ayala (1994 president of the American Association for the Advancement of Science):

> It was Darwin's greatest accomplishment to show that the directive organization of living beings can be explained as the result of a natural process, natural selection, without any need to resort to a Creator or other external agent. . . . Darwin's theory encountered opposition in religious circles, not so much because he proposed the evolutionary origin of living things (which had been proposed many times before, even by Christian theologians), but because his mechanism, natural selection, excluded God as the explanation accounting for the obvious design of organisms.

It is Darwin's mechanism of natural selection that supposedly can account for the otherwise "obvious design of organisms"; thus natural selection functions as a designer substitute. Materialists claim that the Darwinian mechanism is so well established as a creative mechanism that it warrants the exclusion of any consideration of the evidence for intelligent design in the biology classroom. *That's what Darwin has to do with it.*

Does Darwin's mechanism have the power to create bacteria, bears and human beings? Should the evidence for intelligent design continue to be excluded from the biology classroom?

Come along and see how imaginative proponents of the two different stories answer these questions. Inside you'll meet Professor Teller, an advocate of Darwinism, and Professor Questor, who presents evidence for intelligent design in nature. In a frank yet friendly and respectful way, they explain clearly many of the key aspects of this important debate. It's a fun and interesting ride.

Unfortunately, this dispute usually produces more wind than wisdom. We're going to see if we can identify some of the key issues behind all the noise, and see if we can shed some light, not just generate heat.

To tell the story properly, we'll have to go back a few days.

ON TV, THEY MAKE THE PICTURE GO ALL WAVY WHEN THEY DO THE "BACK-IN-TIME" THING!

Sorry. This is a book. You have to do some of the special effects yourself.

4

WELL, I DON'T THINK I'D ARGUE WITH THE FACTS, BUT I'VE BEGUN TO HAVE SOME QUESTIONS ABOUT SOME OF THE CONCLUSIONS...

FACT!

Professor Teller

PROOF! ng Experi PROOF! the P P RO OF log Mam

...AND I GUESS I RESENT BEING LABELED A CRANK OR A NEANDERTHAL JUST BECAUSE I WANT TO ASK SOME QUESTIONS.

OK, IT'S YOUR FUNERAL. IF YOU'RE FREE THIS AFTERNOON, I CAN SET UP A MEETING WITH PROFESSOR TELLER, THE FORUM'S KEYNOTE SPEAKER. YOU CAN GO OVER THE TOPICS THEN.

FACT! FACT

OK.

WHAT AM I GETTING MYSELF INTO?

THAT AFTERNOON, IN THE COMMITTEE MEETING ROOM...

OH BOY, OH BOY! EVOLUTION VS. CREATIONISM! I CAN'T WAIT!

WHOA, THERE! HANG ON A SEC. BEFORE WE GET STARTED, WE'VE GOT TO CLEAR UP SOME TERMS. WORDS CAN BE USED A LOT OF DIFFERENT WAYS.

7

THIS TERM... **...WILL MEAN THIS.**

Creationism *or*
Creation-science

The belief that the earth is no more than 10,000 years old, and that all biological life forms were created in six calendar days and have remained relatively stable throughout their existence.

Intelligent Design *or*
Design Theory

The belief that the earth and biological life owe their existence to a purposeful, intelligent creator.

Darwinism

The belief that undirected mechanistic processes (primarily random mutation and natural selection) can account for all the diverse and complex living organisms that exist. Insists that there is no long range plan or purpose in the history of life (i.e., that changes happen without intent).

THIS TERM...	...WILL MEAN THIS.
Micro-evolution	Refers to minor variations that occur in populations over time. Examples include variation in moth coloration and finch beaks, and the emergence of different breeds of dogs.
Macro-evolution	Refers to the emergence of major innovations or the unguided development of new structures (like wings), new organs (like lungs), and body plans (like the origin of insects and birds). Includes changes above the species level, especially new phyla or classes.
Common descent	The theory that all currently living organisms are descended from a common ancestor.

That's how the discussion got started. That brings us up to the present, and the planning session will start pretty soon.

We aim to please.

Thinking about the story

When somebody says "scientist," what do you typically think of? When somebody calls someone else a "creationist," what do you typically think of?

When a scientist has a debate with a creationist, who usually wins and why?

Have you ever seen such a debate, or is your impression based on how they're portrayed on TV?

15

Those Marvelous Animal Breeders

LONG, LONG AGO, MEN ROAMED THE EARTH, HUNTING ANIMALS FOR FOOD—DEER AND BEAR, BOAR AND BUFFALO.

WHEN THE HUNT WAS SUCCESSFUL, THEY WOULD CAMP, BUTCHER THE KILL, EAT THE MEAT, AND THROW OUT THE SCRAPS AND BONES.

UH, GROG?

ONE NIGHT SOME WOLF-LIKE ANIMALS — NATURAL SCAVENGERS — SLIPPED IN WHILE EVERYONE WAS ASLEEP AND FEASTED ON THE LEFTOVERS.

THIS SOON GOT TO BE A HABIT.

UMM, (SMACK) WE GOTTA COME HERE MORE OFTEN.

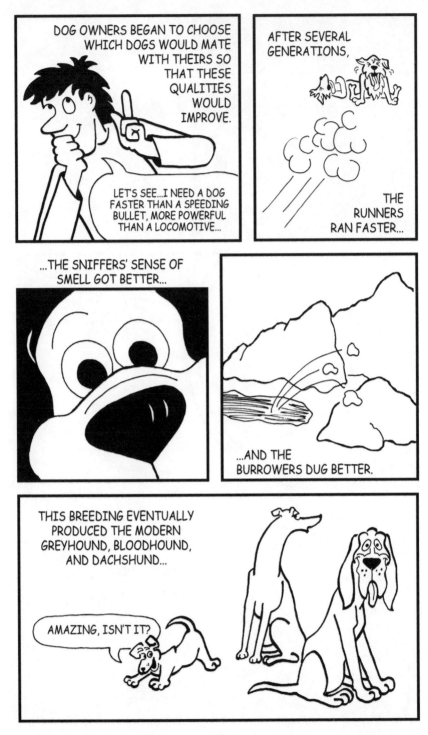

...AS WELL AS LITERALLY HUNDREDS OF OTHER BREEDS.

DARWIN CALLED THIS TYPE OF BREEDING "ARTIFICAL SELECTION."
HE SAID THAT HIS PROPOSED MECHANISM OF "NATURAL SELECTION"
WAS SIMILAR TO ARTIFICIAL SELECTION.

HE REASONED THAT IF MAN HAD BEEN ABLE TO CREATE THESE WONDERS OF THE BIOLOGICAL WORLD IN JUST A FEW DOZEN GENERATIONS...

ARTIFICIAL SELECTION

NATURAL SELECTION

A FEW GENERATIONS

A FEW MILLION YEARS

IMAGINE WHAT NATURE CAN CREATE
OVER MILLIONS OF YEARS.

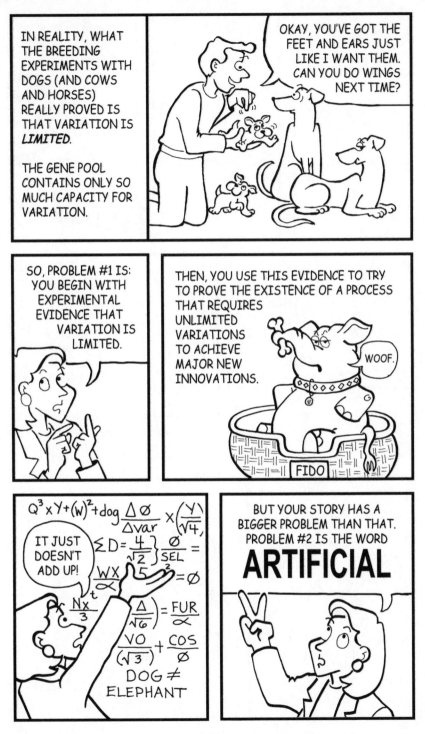

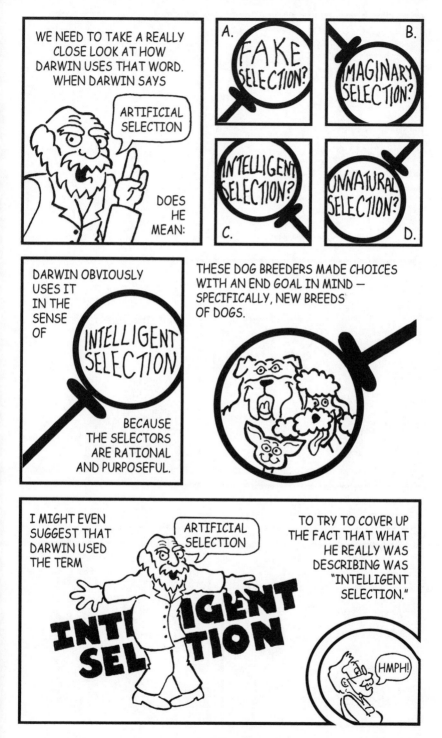

Thinking About the Story

Throughout the rest of this book, we're going to look at some evidence, and we're going to look at the conclusions people draw from that evidence. We want you to start thinking about whether those conclusions make sense. So really, this book is partly about evidence and partly about logic.

To help you begin thinking logically, we'll need to define a couple of terms: "argument" and "fallacy."

You probably think of an argument as two angry people shouting at each other. But that's not the type we're talking about. In the study of logic, an "argument" is a series of statements that tries to prove something.* Here is a classic example of an argument:

All men are mortal.

Socrates was a man.

Therefore, Socrates was mortal.

Words like "therefore" and "so" are very important. They tell you that whatever comes next is justified because of what came before it. In other words, according to some rule of logic, what I'm *about* to say follows from what I *just* said.

A fallacy is an error in reasoning, or a flaw in an argument. Usually it means that the conclusion is not justified by what came before it. Here are some common fallacies:

Faulty Analogy. An inappropriate comparison or the attempt to compare two or more dissimilar things.

Example:

If one man can mow a lawn in two hours, two men can mow it in an hour.

OK so far... but watch!

---

* For those of you who are looking for extra credit, the "something" you're trying to prove is usually called a *proposition* or a *conclusion*.

Therefore, if one plane can cross the Atlantic in two hours, two planes should be able to cross it in an hour.

Extension. Taking a line of reasoning to its extreme.

Example: "Senator Phogg was elected according to the law of the land. If you question his integrity, pretty soon you'll be questioning the very foundation of our government."

There are many types of fallacies. Some of them are humorous, and some are very subtle. You don't need to know what type of fallacy it is. All you have to do is recognize it.

See if you can identify what's wrong with the following arguments.

"If it's raining, there must be clouds.

There are clouds.

Therefore, it must be raining."

"If I am elected, I promise to reduce crime. I will reduce crime by making fewer things illegal."

Application

1) Did you see any of these fallacies in the last chapter?

2) One scientist recently said,

"You can't accept one part of science because it brings you good things like electricity and penicillin, and throw away another part because it brings you some things you don't like about the origin of life."

How is he making a "wagon word" out of the word *science*?

Now we will rejoin Professor Teller and Professor Questor as they continue to prepare for the forum.

The Moths Who Changed Their Colors

*O*nce upon a time in merry old England...

... THERE WERE TWO KINDS OF MOTHS.

THEY WERE BOTH CALLED "PEPPERED MOTHS" (BY THOSE WHO CALLED THEM ANYTHING) BUT WERE DISTINGUISHED AS *BISTON BETULARIA TYPICA* AND *BISTON BETULARIA CARBONARIA* BY THE WISE MEN.

LIKE PEPPER, THEY WERE SPOTTED BLACK AND WHITE - ONE KIND WAS MOSTLY WHITE WITH SOME BLACK SPOTS, THE OTHER MOSTLY BLACK WITH SOME WHITE SPOTS.

THE MOTHS WERE APPARENTLY APPRECIATED FOR THEIR FLAVOR BY THE LOCAL BIRDS, WHO GOBBLED THEM UP WHENEVER THEY WERE HUNGRY.

YIPES!

HOWEVER, BIRDS DON'T CHASE WHAT THEY CAN'T SEE. LOTS OF TREES IN THAT KINGDOM WERE COVERED WITH LICHEN (A GREENISH-GRAY GROWTH THAT OFTEN COVERS ROCKS AND TREES).

32

THE LIGHTER MOTHS WERE WELL CAMOUFLAGED, SINCE THEY WERE JUST ABOUT THE SAME COLOR AS THE LICHEN.

THE DARKER VARIETY STOOD OUT LIKE... LIKE ... WELL, LIKE DARK MOTHS ON A LIGHT BACKGROUND.

I THINK I SEE A PROBLEM, HERE.

AS A RESULT, SOON THERE WERE VERY FEW BLACK BISTONS AROUND.

YES, I DO SEE A PROBLEM, HERE.

AND THAT'S THE WAY IT REMAINED FOR A VERY, VERY LONG TIME.

BUT SOMETHING HAPPENED THAT CHANGED ALL THIS.

COUGH!

MEN IN THE MIDDLE PARTS OF THAT REALM BEGAN TO BURN COAL IN HUGE FACTORY FURNACES. THIS BLACKENED THE SKY WITH SMOKE.

AFTER A WHILE, THE SMOKE KILLED MOST OF THE LICHEN AND LAID A GRIMY BLACK SOOT ON HOUSE AND HILL, ROCK AND TREE.

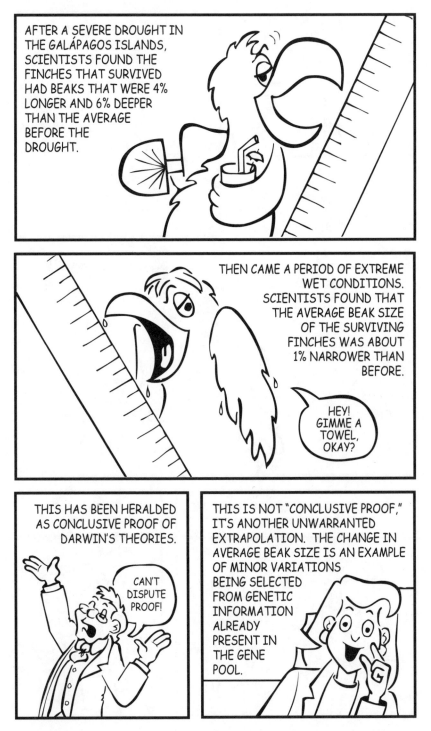

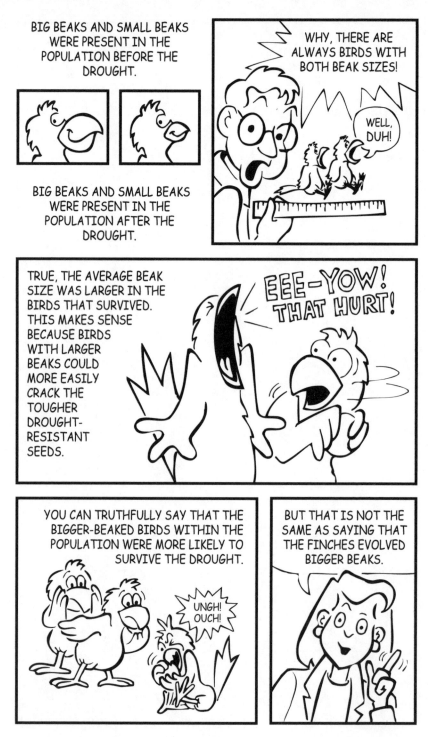

41

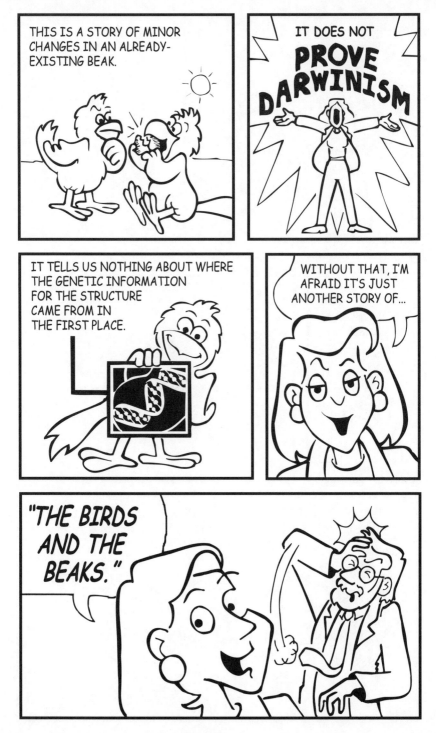

Thinking About the Story

Arguments and Fallacies (again!)

Think of arguments as having two types of sentences. One type of sentence is what someone is trying to prove. Sometimes people call this the *conclusion* of the argument. The second type of sentence is supposed to contain the reasons or the justification for what someone is trying to prove. People sometimes call this type of sentence a *premise*. (An argument can have several premises.)

Sometimes you see a fallacy when somebody goofs up the form of the argument. (The form is how you put an argument together.) For example, one very reliable form of argument looks like this:

If A is true, then B is true.
A is true.
Therefore, B is true.

Now, think of the example we used earlier.

If it is raining, then there are clouds.

There are clouds.

Therefore, it is raining.

Can you spot the mistake? Let's look at it from a logical point of view.

If it is raining (If A is true), then there are clouds (then B is true). So far, so good.

There are clouds (B is true).

Therefore, it is raining (Therefore A is true).

This is called a "formal" fallacy, because it is an error in the *form* of the argument. If the fallacy is *in*formal, that means the mistake is in the content of the argument (not in its form).

To beg or not to beg

In the last story, you heard about the fallacy of Begging the Question. That may have sounded strange, since nobody seemed to be begging for anything. However, one definition of beg is "to assume without proof."

In the study of logic, to Beg the Question is to make one statement and then "prove" it by repeating the statement using slightly different words.

For example,

"We have made tremendous progress in our investigation of the robbery. We can now say without a doubt that it was committed by thieves."

"You should give us a bigger allowance. If you would only give us as much allowance as we ask for, we wouldn't have to ask you for more money."

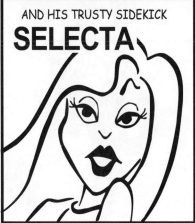

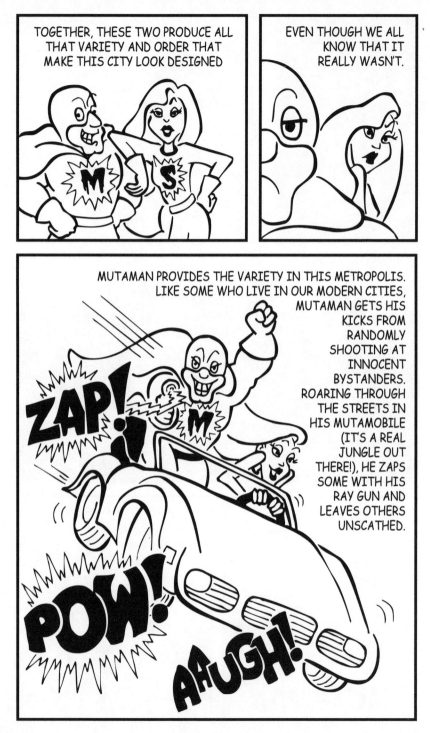

TOGETHER, THESE TWO PRODUCE ALL THAT VARIETY AND ORDER THAT MAKE THIS CITY LOOK DESIGNED

EVEN THOUGH WE ALL KNOW THAT IT REALLY WASN'T.

MUTAMAN PROVIDES THE VARIETY IN THIS METROPOLIS. LIKE SOME WHO LIVE IN OUR MODERN CITIES, MUTAMAN GETS HIS KICKS FROM RANDOMLY SHOOTING AT INNOCENT BYSTANDERS. ROARING THROUGH THE STREETS IN HIS MUTAMOBILE (IT'S A REAL JUNGLE OUT THERE!), HE ZAPS SOME WITH HIS RAY GUN AND LEAVES OTHERS UNSCATHED.

ZAP!

POW!

AAUGH!

49

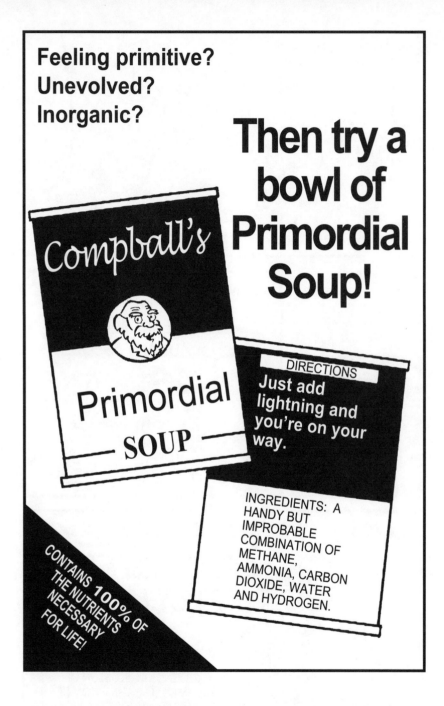

NOW THE SCENE SHIFTS TO MUTAMAN'S BEAUTIFUL AND SAGACIOUS PARTNER, *NATURA SELECTA.*

SELECTA (AS SHE PREFERS TO BE CALLED) BRINGS ORDER OUT OF ALL THE CHAOS THAT MUTAMAN PRODUCES.

SHE CAREFULLY SCRUTINIZES EACH ZAPPED MUTANT TO DECIDE WHETHER THE MUTANT IS MORE FIT THAN BEFORE.

IF IT IS, SELECTA WAVES HER POWER WAND AND THE "REPRODUCTION PERMIT BADGE" BECOMES LARGER AND MORE POWERFUL.

SHE MAKES NO OBSERVABLE CHANGES IN THOSE WITH NEUTRAL MUTATIONS.

AND IF THE MUTANT IS NOT AS FIT AS BEFORE, SHE EITHER MAKES THE BADGE SMALLER OR REMOVES IT ENTIRELY.

I CAN'T BELIEVE IT... AFTER ALL THIS TIME AT THE TOP OF THE FOOD CHAIN... I THOUGHT IT COULD NEVER HAPPEN TO ME...

MUTANTS WITH MORE POWERFUL BADGES PRODUCE MORE OFFSPRING IN THEIR PARTICULAR NEIGHBORHOOD. THIS CHANGES THE POPULATION OF THE NEIGHBORHOOD AND EVENTUALLY CHANGES THE WHOLE CHARACTER OF THE CITY.

WHOA! DID I MISS SOMETHING?

YOU SURE DID, OL' BUDDY. WE BOTH DID.

DON'T WORRY! THEY'LL BE GONE SOON!

WITH THESE TWO SUPERHEROES, ALL OF THIS DIVERSE LIFE ON EARTH HAS DEVELOPED FROM ONE OR A FEW SIMPLE LIFE FORMS.

SCIENTISTS STILL ARGUE WHETHER MUTAMAN'S WORK IS SUCCESSFUL ONLY IN THE CASE OF VERY SMALL CHANGES...

SMALL? YOU COULD HIDE ALL OF GALÁPAGOS IN THAT BEAK!

53

Little Jumps, Big Jumps

Adapted from *Darwin's Black Box* by Michael Behe.

Suppose you have a 4-foot ditch in your back yard, stretching from horizon to horizon. This ditch separates your back yard from your neighbor's. If one day you found your neighbor in your yard and asked how he got there, you would have no reason to doubt him if he answered, "I jumped over the ditch."

If the ditch were 8 feet wide and he gave the same answer, you would be impressed with his athletic ability.

If the ditch were 15 feet wide, you might become suspicious and ask him to jump again while you watched. If he said he couldn't because he had sprained his knee when he landed, you would have your doubts, but you couldn't be certain.

Suppose the "ditch" were actually a canyon 100 feet wide. You wouldn't believe for a moment that he had jumped over.

But suppose your neighbor modifies his claim...

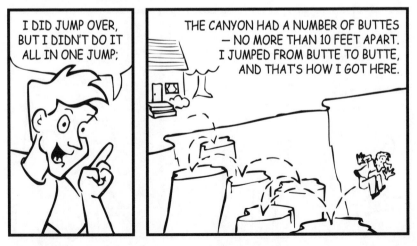

I DID JUMP OVER, BUT I DIDN'T DO IT ALL IN ONE JUMP;

THE CANYON HAD A NUMBER OF BUTTES — NO MORE THAN 10 FEET APART. I JUMPED FROM BUTTE TO BUTTE, AND THAT'S HOW I GOT HERE.

55

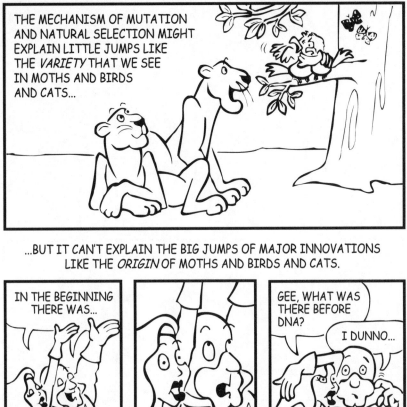

THE MECHANISM OF MUTATION AND NATURAL SELECTION MIGHT EXPLAIN LITTLE JUMPS LIKE THE *VARIETY* THAT WE SEE IN MOTHS AND BIRDS AND CATS...

...BUT IT CAN'T EXPLAIN THE BIG JUMPS OF MAJOR INNOVATIONS LIKE THE *ORIGIN* OF MOTHS AND BIRDS AND CATS.

IN THE BEGINNING THERE WAS...

GEE, WHAT WAS THERE BEFORE DNA?

I DUNNO...

BUT THAT'S MUTATION'S JOB, TO REARRANGE THE DNA TO GET NEW STRUCTURES.

YOU CAN CREATE *VARIATION* WHEN THE EXISTING DNA GETS SHUFFLED.

YES, BUT EVEN IN ENGLISH IT'S POSSIBLE TO TAKE SOME WORDS AND READ THEM BACKWARDS TO MAKE COMPLETELY NEW MEANING. HERE'S AN EXAMPLE...

CHRISTMAS COMES MERRILY? HO HO, SAY I. HUNGRY BIRDS; NO FIRES CRACKLING. RENTS HIGH, NOT PAID. LONG BILLS; EMPTY BARNS. NO PEACE AND PROSPERITY.

NOW, WATCH THIS...

PROSPERITY AND PEACE! NO BARNS EMPTY. BILLS LONG PAID; NOT-HIGH RENTS. CRACKLING FIRES; NO BIRDS HUNGRY. I SAY, "HO HO!" MERRILY COMES CHRISTMAS!

VERY CLEVER! BUT THESE WORD PLAYS DON'T HAPPEN BY ACCIDENT. IT TAKES EFFORT AND INGENUITY TO CREATE A PARAGRAPH THAT ALSO MAKES SENSE WHEN IT'S REVERSED.

MUTATION, ON THE OTHER HAND, IS RANDOM. THE LINES OF GENETIC CODE MUTATE RANDOMLY.

THERE ARE POINT MUTATIONS, DUPLICATIONS, CROSSES, DOUBLINGS, INVERSIONS...

THEN YOU HAVE THE PROBABILITY PROBLEM. NEW STRUCTURES DON'T JUST TAKE A SENTENCE'S WORTH OF NEW GENETIC CODE, THEY TAKE A WHOLE SET OF ENCYCLOPEDIAS' WORTH.

WHAT ARE THE CHANCES THAT YOU COULD DECOMPILE A WORD-PROCESSING PROGRAM, SHUFFLE THE LINES OF CODE AT RANDOM, RECOMPILE IT AND GET A GRAPHICS PROGRAM?

BEEP! IN YOUR DREAMS!

MUTATION MIGHT EXPLAIN THE *VARIETY* THAT WE SEE IN SPECIES.

VIVA LA DIFFERENCE!

BUT THOSE ARE SMALL CHANGES, NOT LARGE.

AND NATURAL SELECTION CAN EXPLAIN THE SURVIVAL OF A SPECIES.

MAYBE WE OUGHT TO HELP HIM?

UNGH! HUNUGH!

NOT ONLY THAT, BUT THE LIMBS HAVE A PARALLEL BONE STRUCTURE EVEN WHEN THEY ARE USED FOR VERY DIFFERENT PURPOSES.

IN DOGS AND HORSES, THE FORELIMB IS ALSO A LEG, JUST AS A HIND LIMB IS. BUT IN HUMANS, IT'S AN ARM AND IT'S NOT USUALLY USED FOR WALKING.

IN A BIRD, IT'S A WING, USED FOR FLYING AND BALANCE.

IN A WHALE, IT'S A FLIPPER (USED FOR FLIPPING).

YET THE ARRANGEMENT OF THE BONES IN THESE LIMBS IS STRIKINGLY SIMILAR. IT SUGGESTS THAT ALL THESE ANIMALS ARE DESCENDED FROM A COMMON ANCESTOR.

WE'LL LOOK AT YOUR ARM, SINCE IT'S HANDY... (OR SHOULD IT BE "ARM-Y"?)

YOUR UPPER ARM (DOCTORS CALL IT THE HUMERUS) IS A SINGLE BONE. SAME THING FOR DOGS, HORSES, BIRDS, WHALES (AND YOUR LEG).

BELOW YOUR ELBOW IS YOUR LOWER ARM. THIS HAS TWO BONES SIDE-BY-SIDE (RADIUS AND ULNA); SAME WITH DOGS, ETC. (AND YOUR LEG).

THEN COME THE WRIST BONES (EIGHT CARPALS IN HUMANS); THESE OTHER ANIMALS HAVE SOMETHING SIMILAR, THOUGH OFTEN WITH FEWER BONES.

YOUR ANKLE AND HEEL AREA HAVE THE SAME SORT OF THING.

THEN YOU HAVE FIVE "STRINGS" OF BONES IN YOUR THUMB AND FINGERS (METATARSALS AND PHALANGES). THE OTHER ANIMALS ARE SIMILAR, THOUGH OFTEN WITH FEWER "TOES."

THE HORSE HAS ONLY ONE TOE ON EACH FOOT, AND RUNS ON HIS "FINGERNAILS"!

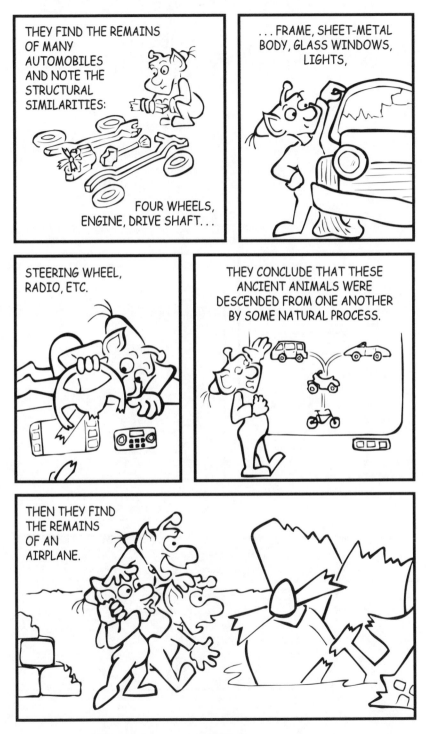

69

Thinking About the Story

We've already talked about two important parts of an argument: the premise and the conclusion. Here's another way to approach the study of logical arguments. Some people who study logic will tell you that it's helpful to be more specific about what a premise does. These logicians (as they are called) would say that one type of premise provides evidence, while another type of premise shows why the evidence is important.

In other words, evidence is a type of premise that gives information that specifically supports the conclusion. The other type of premise (called a warrant) shows how the evidence connects to the conclusion. Have you ever heard someone talking about an "unwarranted" conclusion? That means a conclusion that is not supported by evidence or connected to the evidence.

The conclusion, evidence, and warrant can occur in any order. Think about our earlier example:

All men are mortal. (This is the evidence.)

Socrates was a man. (This is the warrant. It is saying that Socrates is an example of a group we call "men.")

Therefore, Socrates was mortal. (This is the conclusion.)

Sometimes the best way to try to identify a fallacy is to break the argument into these three pieces. Then ask yourself if it really makes sense. Think about the following story about a man telling a friend about a hunting trip he's just taken.

Is the Panda's Thumb a Dumb Design?

ACCORDING TO STEPHEN JAY GOULD, THE PANDA'S THUMB IS PROOF OF DARWINISM.

IMPERFECT DESIGN PROVES THAT THE CREATIVE POWER AT WORK IS NOT INTELLIGENT.

THE GIANT PANDA IS A BEAR-LIKE CREATURE, AN ENDANGERED SPECIES WITH ONLY ABOUT A THOUSAND LEFT IN THE WILDS OF NEPAL AND CHINA. IT EATS THE LEAVES, STEMS AND ROOTS OF THE BAMBOO PLANT.

OPPOSABLE THUMBS (LIKE HUMANS AND APES HAVE) ARE USEFUL FOR GRASPING. GOULD POINTS OUT THAT THE PANDA'S THUMB (WHICH IT USES TO STRIP LEAVES OFF THE BAMBOO PLANT) IS NOT A TRUE THUMB AT ALL. IT'S A WRIST BONE THAT HAS BEEN ENLARGED AND GIVEN A SET OF MUSCLES TO DO SOMETHING SIMILAR.

GOULD SAYS THAT THE PANDA'S EVOLUTIONARY HISTORY RULED OUT THE "ENGINEER'S BEST SOLUTION" TO THIS PROBLEM. HE SAYS THAT PANDA'S "TRUE THUMB" WAS ALREADY COMMITTED TO ANOTHER ROLE — SINCE IT'S ON THE FRONT PAW OF AN ANIMAL THAT WALKS ON ALL FOUR FEET.

ONE... TWO... THREE... FOUR...

SO THE PANDA HAD TO USE WHATEVER PARTS WERE AVAILABLE AND "SETTLE FOR AN ENLARGED WRIST BONE — A SOMEWHAT CLUMSY, BUT WORKABLE, SOLUTION."

HEY! WHO'S CLUMSY?

THE EXISTENCE OF "ODD ARRANGEMENTS" AND "FUNNY SOLUTIONS" TO THE VARIOUS ENGINEERING PROBLEMS IN NATURE SHOWS US THAT A BLIND, NATURAL PROCESS LIKE DARWINISM HAS BEEN AT WORK RATHER THAN A "SENSIBLE GOD."

I HAVE THREE PROBLEMS WITH YOUR STORY.

FIRST, I HAVE A PERSONAL OBJECTION. I'D LIKE TO QUOTE THE GREEK PHILOSOPHER DIOGENES WHEN HE DISCUSSED HOW TO PERCEIVE INTELLIGENCE IN DESIGN. HE SAID THAT...

"THE REGULARITY OF THE SEASONS WOULD NOT HAVE BEEN POSSIBLE WITHOUT INTELLIGENCE, THAT ALL THINGS SHOULD HAVE THEIR MEASURE: WINTER AND SUMMER AND NIGHT AND DAY...[WHICH] IF ONE WILL STUDY THEM WILL BE FOUND TO HAVE THE BEST POSSIBLE ARRANGEMENT."

"BEST POSSIBLE ARRANGEMENT," INDEED! THAT'S RIDICULOUS!

YOU CAN'T CALL IT "DESIGN" JUST BECAUSE IT HAPPENS TO FIT YOUR IDEA OF THE WAY IT OUGHT TO BE!

MY POINT EXACTLY!

JUST BECAUSE THE THUMB DOESN'T FIT GOULD'S IDEA OF WHAT A THUMB SHOULD BE, HOW CAN HE CONCLUDE THAT IT ISN'T DESIGNED?

IN A FEW MINUTES THEY WERE SEATED IN THE OFFICE OF
THE CURATOR, SIR RICHARD HAVERSHAM.

81

NEXT, WE INTERVIEWED ONE SIR JULIAN HUXLEY. HE CLAIMED THE MR. DARWIN WAS MISTAKEN ABOUT THE NUMBER OF FOSSILS STOLEN.

THE TRANSITIONAL FOSSILS, SAID HE, WERE REALLY RATHER FEW IN NUMBER. THEY ARE MISSING BECAUSE ALL BIG CHANGES IN LIVING THINGS TOOK PLACE IN SMALL, ISOLATED GROUPS THAT WOULD HAVE A LESSER CHANCE OF LEAVING FOSSILS.

HE THOUGHT THE MISSING FOSSILS HADN'T YET BEEN REMOVED FROM THE PREMISES, BUT HAD BEEN HIDDEN IN VARIOUS CLOSETS BY ONE OF THE CUSTODIANS, POP SMALL.

HE THOUGHT THAT A CAREFUL SEARCH OF ALL THE CLOSETS WOULD PROBABLY TURN THEM UP.

CRASH!

I SAID *CAREFUL!*

83

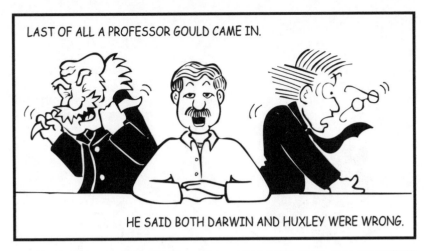

LAST OF ALL A PROFESSOR GOULD CAME IN.

HE SAID BOTH DARWIN AND HUXLEY WERE WRONG.

THE MUSEUM HAD NO RECORD OF HAVING EVER HAD ANY OF THESE ALLEGED FOSSILS. NEITHER DID ANY OF THE OTHER MUSEUMS OF WHICH HE WAS AWARE. HE SAID THERE WERE STILL ABOUT 1/4 BILLION FOSSILS CATALOGUED IN ALL THESE COLLECTIONS, AND THAT ALL THE MUSEUMS SEEMED TO BE MISSING THE SAME FOSSILS.

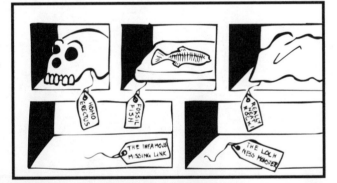

IT MUST HAVE BEEN A VERY CLEVER THIEF WHO COULD GET INTO ALL THE MUSEUMS AND STEAL SO MANY FOSSILS, PLUS JUST THE RIGHT PAGES FROM THEIR REGISTRATION BOOKS SO AS NOT TO LEAVE ANY RECORD!

HE POINTED OUT THAT ALL THE EXISTING FOSSIL COLLECTIONS SHOW PLANTS AND ANIMALS THAT APPEAR ON THE SCENE FULLY FORMED, SEEM TO REMAIN RELATIVELY UNCHANGED FOR SOME MILLIONS OF YEARS, AND THEN DISAPPEAR.

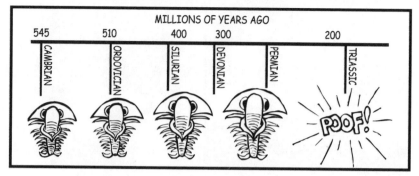

HE SUGGESTED THAT THE CHANGES HAD TAKEN PLACE RAPIDLY - NOT SLOWLY - THROUGH A MYSTERIOUS PROCESS HE CALLED "PUNCTUATION." THEREFORE, THERE WERE NEVER MANY TRANSITION ANIMALS, AND THUS FEW OR NO MISSING FOSSILS.

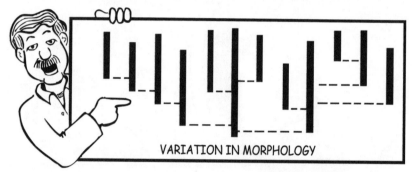

VARIATION IN MORPHOLOGY

WHEN HE HAD LEFT, ALL EYES TURNED TO THE CELEBRATED DETECTIVE.

WHAT DO YOU THINK, HOLMES? I CAN MAKE NEITHER HEAD NOR TAIL OF IT!

I THINK THEY'RE ALL MISTAKEN, THOUGH PROFESSOR GOULD IS AT LEAST ON THE RIGHT TRACK.

HOW CAN YOU SAY THAT, MR. HOLMES?

WELL, FIRST OF ALL, I'M NOT SURE WE CAN TRULY CALL THEM "MISSING FOSSILS."

NOT ONE OF THESE MEN, NOR YOU YOURSELF HAVE EVER SEEN THE FOSSILS, AS PROFESSOR GOULD POINTED OUT. BY THEIR OWN ADMISSION, NONE OF THESE MEN WERE EYEWITNESSES TO THE ALLEGED ROBBERY.

SECOND, I KNOW E. ROSION'S CRIMINAL RECORD. HE IS VERY UNDISCRIMINATING AS A BURGLAR. I HARDLY THINK HE WOULD KNOW ENOUGH TO STEAL JUST THE TRANSITIONAL FOSSILS WHILE LEAVING ALL THESE OTHERS BEHIND.

86

Thinking About the Story

Does this story remind you of the hunting dog that climbs trees?

My dog can climb trees. If you don't believe me, I'll show you the tree.

The fossil record proves that all life forms are constantly changing. If you don't believe me, I'll show you the parts that have remained unchanged.

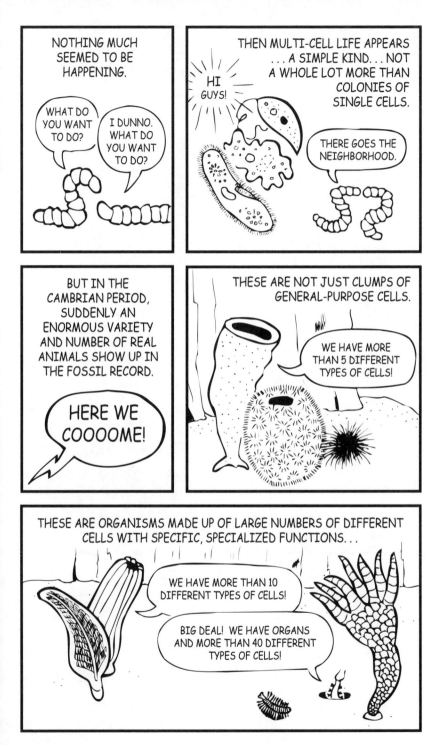

ORGANIZED AROUND SOME FIFTY DIFFERENT BODY-PLANS WITH DIGESTIVE, LOCOMOTIVE, SENSORY, GUIDANCE, AND WEAPONS SYSTEMS, AND SOME WITH SHELLS!

OUT OF OUR WAY! WE HAVE ORGANS AND 50 TYPES OF CELLS!

SO? I HAVE ORGANS, 60 TYPES OF CELLS AND MY RELATIVES HAVE A BACKBONE!

BECAUSE SO MANY COMPLEX ANIMAL DESIGNS BURST INTO THE FOSSIL RECORD SO SUDDENLY, SCIENTISTS CALL IT

THE CAMBRIAN EXPLOSION

MEASUREMENTS OF THE AGE OF CAMBRIAN ROCKS USING SOPHISTICATED NEW TECHNIQUES SHOW THAT THE CAMBRIAN EXPLOSION LASTED LESS THAN 10 MILLION YEARS. . . LONG TO US, BUT VERY RAPID IN GEOLOGICAL TIME.

GEOLOGICAL TIME

CAMBRIAN EXPLOSION

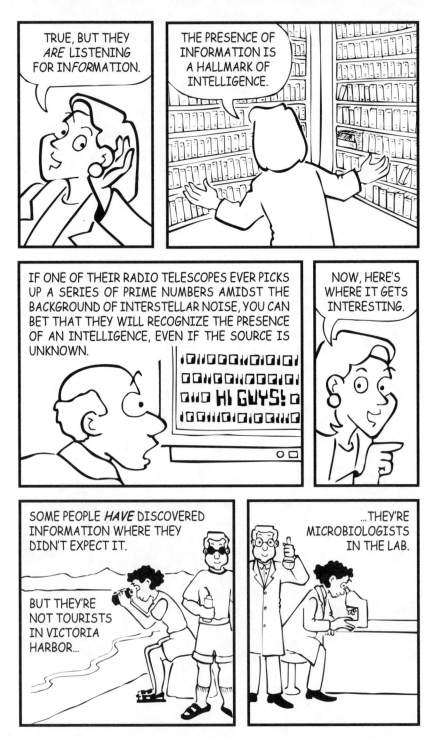

TRUE, BUT THEY *ARE* LISTENING FOR INFORMATION.

THE PRESENCE OF INFORMATION IS A HALLMARK OF INTELLIGENCE.

IF ONE OF THEIR RADIO TELESCOPES EVER PICKS UP A SERIES OF PRIME NUMBERS AMIDST THE BACKGROUND OF INTERSTELLAR NOISE, YOU CAN BET THAT THEY WILL RECOGNIZE THE PRESENCE OF AN INTELLIGENCE, EVEN IF THE SOURCE IS UNKNOWN.

HI GUYS!

NOW, HERE'S WHERE IT GETS INTERESTING.

SOME PEOPLE *HAVE* DISCOVERED INFORMATION WHERE THEY DIDN'T EXPECT IT.

BUT THEY'RE NOT TOURISTS IN VICTORIA HARBOR...

...THEY'RE MICROBIOLOGISTS IN THE LAB.

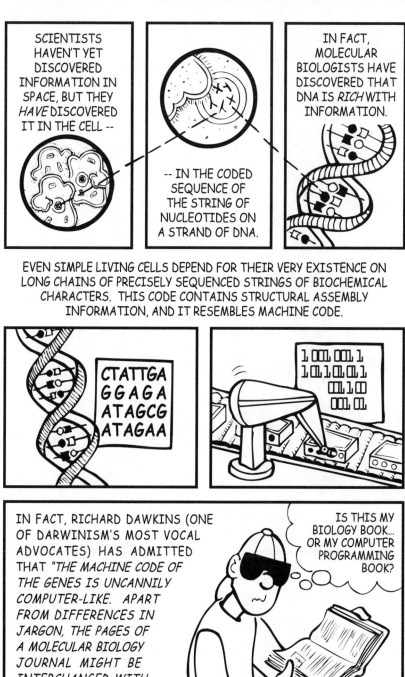

SCIENTISTS HAVEN'T YET DISCOVERED INFORMATION IN SPACE, BUT THEY *HAVE* DISCOVERED IT IN THE CELL --

-- IN THE CODED SEQUENCE OF THE STRING OF NUCLEOTIDES ON A STRAND OF DNA.

IN FACT, MOLECULAR BIOLOGISTS HAVE DISCOVERED THAT DNA IS *RICH* WITH INFORMATION.

EVEN SIMPLE LIVING CELLS DEPEND FOR THEIR VERY EXISTENCE ON LONG CHAINS OF PRECISELY SEQUENCED STRINGS OF BIOCHEMICAL CHARACTERS. THIS CODE CONTAINS STRUCTURAL ASSEMBLY INFORMATION, AND IT RESEMBLES MACHINE CODE.

CTATTGA
GGAGA
ATAGCG
ATAGAA

IN FACT, RICHARD DAWKINS (ONE OF DARWINISM'S MOST VOCAL ADVOCATES) HAS ADMITTED THAT "*THE MACHINE CODE OF THE GENES IS UNCANNILY COMPUTER-LIKE. APART FROM DIFFERENCES IN JARGON, THE PAGES OF A MOLECULAR BIOLOGY JOURNAL MIGHT BE INTERCHANGED WITH THOSE OF A COMPUTER ENGINEERING JOURNAL.*"

IS THIS MY BIOLOGY BOOK... OR MY COMPUTER PROGRAMMING BOOK?

115

116

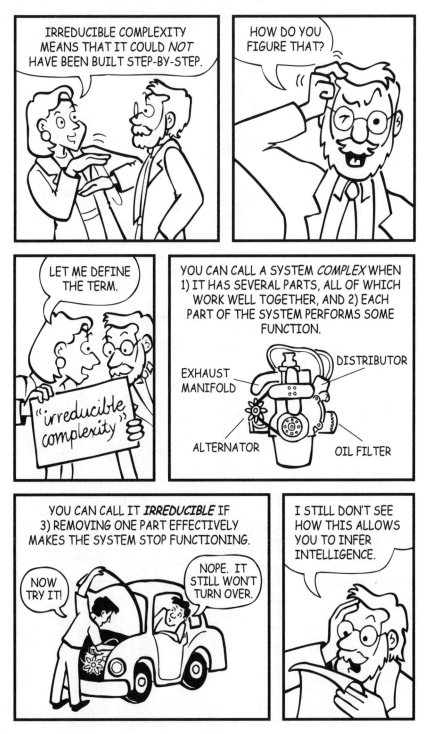

WHY COULDN'T THIS MOLECULAR MOTOR HAVE EVOLVED?

THINK OF THE COMMON HOUSEHOLD MOUSETRAP.*

IT HAS A BASE, A SPRING, A HAMMER, A TRIGGER, A HOLDING BAR, AND A COUPLE OF STAPLES

IF ONLY HALF THE PARTS ARE IN PLACE, THAT DOESN'T MEAN IT WILL ONLY CATCH HALF THE NUMBER OF MICE. IT WON'T CATCH *ANY*. A MOUSETRAP IS IRREDUCIBLY COMPLEX.

JUST LIKE THE MOUSETRAP, THE INTRICATE MACHINERY IN THIS MOLECULAR MOTOR INCLUDES MANY DISCRETE PARTS: A ROTOR, A STATOR, O-RINGS, BUSHINGS, AND A DRIVE SHAFT. OVER 20 COMPLEX PROTEIN PARTS. THE CELL ALSO NEEDS *ANOTHER* 20 COMPLEX PROTEINS TO ASSEMBLE THE MOTOR.

IF ANY ONE OF THESE PROTEINS IS MISSING, THE MOTOR WON'T WORK!

* ADAPTED FROM MICHAEL BEHE'S <u>DARWIN'S BLACK BOX</u>.

121

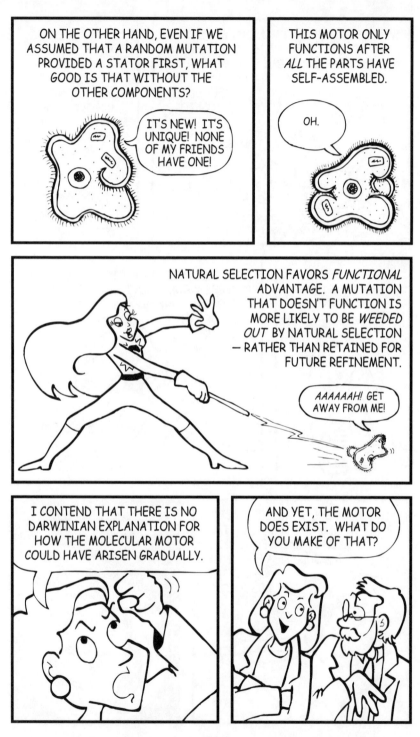

124

125

DARWINISM AT LEAST SEEMS LIKE IT'S STRUGGLING HONESTLY TO FIND THE TRUTH.

I UNDERSTAND YOUR HESITATION, BUT LET ME SEE IF I CAN EXPLAIN WHY I DISAGREE.

FIRST, IF LIFE *IS* THE RESULT OF INTELLIGENT DESIGN, THEN GIVING UP ON TRYING TO FIND A PURELY NATURALISTIC EXPLANATION IS LIKE GIVING UP ON TRYING TO TURN LEAD INTO GOLD. IT'S PROGRESS, NOT DEFEAT.

LEO, MY BOY, THIS IS POINTLESS.

MAYBE I'LL TAKE UP PAINTING.

SECOND, AS FAR AS WHETHER DARWINISM IS "STRUGGLING TO FIND THE TRUTH."

"STRUGGLING," MAYBE. BUT LET ME TELL YOU ONE LAST STORY.

The Case of the Usual Suspects

I WAS READING MY MEDICAL JOURNAL IN OUR BAKER STREET FLAT WHEN HOLMES CAME IN.

HE WAS CARRYING AN EDITION OF THE MORNING PAPER WHICH CONTAINED A SENSATIONAL STORY OF THE MURDER OF PROFESSOR HANNIBAL.

FAMOUS PROFESSOR MURDERED!

YOU DON'T MEAN ALPHONSE HANNIBAL, THE FAMOUS BIG-GAME HUNTER?

131

133

Background Information

Introduction: Darwinism vs. Intelligent Design

Definitions are important. The *Science Framework for California Schools* (1990) says that "the process of teaching science requires a precise, unambiguous use of language" (p. 14) and "scientists, teachers, and students must communicate the definitions of scientific terms and use them with consistency" (p. 17). We agree. Such precise and accurate use of terms is a must if we are to understand one another, especially when discussing a controversial topic like evolution.

One leading high school biology text defines *evolution* as "the process by which modern organisms have descended from ancient organisms" but also "any change in the gene pool of a population" (Miller and Levine, *Biology* [Englewood Cliffs, N.J.: Prentice-Hall, 1993, 1995 and 1998 editions], ref. p. 29). By this definition, *evolution* means *both* the whole creation process *and* any minor change in a population, such as some fruit flies' breeding in August rather than June. It's all evolution! The danger here is that any evidence for minor change becomes evidence for the whole creation story, because it is all "evolution." This only tends to confuse the issue.

In addition, when Miller and Levine discuss major body plans of animals, they assure the students that "evolution works without plan or purpose" and that "evolution is random and undirected" (p. 658). But the text fails to provide any evidence to support these beliefs. Miller has promised John Wiester (in 1996 and again in 1998) that such unwarranted statements will be deleted from future editions.

Another case where the word *evolution* is used equivocally is the *1995 Position Statement* of the National Association of Biology Teachers (NABT). The NABT claimed, "The diversity of life on earth is the outcome of evolution: an unsupervised, impersonal, unpredictable and natural process of temporal descent with genetic modification that is affected by natural selection, chance, historical contingencies and changing environments"

(*The American Biology Teacher,* January 1996, pp. 61-62). In other words, life on earth owes its existence to "evolution," an unsupervised, impersonal process. Yet the NABT statement also failed to provide supporting evidence for this claim. These words were deleted from the statement in 1998 by the NABT after they were publicly criticized by supporters of design theory and professional philosophers.

The most important point of this chapter is that we should never use the E-word without qualification. *Evolution* can mean anything from the changing design of autos (a fact) to the belief that we are here as the result of an accidental process (a speculation unsupported by scientific evidence). Note Professor Teller's glee over the prospect of debating "evolution versus creationism." He has already won the debate by setting its terms as a battle of "science" versus "religious belief," a stereotype widely presented in the media and popularized in the play and film *Inherit the Wind.* To avoid this problem, some would propose using the terms *evolutionism* and *creationism,* where both get an "ism" added to show they are beliefs. But both are heavily loaded "wagon-words" that will lead to misunderstanding. In the next chapter Professor Questor will quite correctly suggest that the debate should be set as Darwinism versus intelligent design.

Darwinism proposes that the "obvious design of organisms" is an illusion because the real creator is Darwin's mechanism of natural selection. This is clear in the quote by 1994 American Association for the Advancement of Science (AAAS) president Francisco J. Ayala in our introduction (p. vi). Reference for this quote is from Francisco J. Ayala, "Darwin's Revolution," in *Creative Evolution!?* ed. J. H. Campbell and J. W. Schopf (Sudbury, Mass.: Jones & Bartlett, 1994), pp. 4-5.

The meaning of *creationism* and *creation science* were clearly defined by the Committee on Science and Creationism of the National Academy of Sciences (NAS) in their 1984 edition of *Science and Creationism: A View from the National Academy of Sciences.* They were defined as including "the following judgments: (1) the earth and universe are relatively young, perhaps only 6,000 to 10,000 years old; (2) the present physical form of the earth can be explained by 'catastrophism,' including a worldwide flood;

and (3) all living things (including humans) were created miraculously, essentially in the forms we now find them" (p. 7).

The 1999 (2nd edition) of this booklet has redefined *creationism* and *creation science* to include both those who hold "old earth" views and those who cite evidence for "intelligent design" (p. 7). The 1999 edition then proceeds as it did in the 1984 edition to cite evidence against only the "young earth" view.

One method of preserving a monopoly and avoiding reasoned debate is by using the tactic of name-calling and false labeling. While a familiar feature of politics, it is unfortunate that the NAS has lent its prestigious name to such an untruthful maneuver. Design theory is not derived from religious authority nor from appeals to Scripture. Like Darwinism, intelligent design theory is a scientific inference derived from biological evidence. The question to be debated is which theory best fits this evidence.

Planning Session

See the notes for "Darwinism vs. Intelligent Design" and the definitions of terms on pages 10-11. Notice how easy it is to slip back into using *evolution* with its various (and ambiguous) meanings instead of distinguishing between *evolution* and *Darwinism.*

Those Marvelous Animal Breeders

Professor Teller's technique of using "artificial selection" as his analogy to validate the mechanism of natural selection was Darwin's own approach. Darwin was impressed by the wide variety of pigeons that had been produced by selective breeding. Indeed, practically every biology textbook uses this same example both to explain and to make convincing their case for natural selection. Yet "artificial selection" is really intelligent, purposeful selection, aiming toward a goal the selector has in mind. This is never mentioned. Nor are any of the other serious problems, both logical and scientific, with this analogy.

Even leading scientists can be blinded in this matter. Francis Crick, winner of the Nobel prize for his discovery of the structure of DNA, says,

136

If you doubt the power of natural selection, I urge you, to save your soul, to read Richard Dawkins's book *[The Blind Watchmaker]*. I think you will find it a revelation. Dawkins gives a nice argument to show how far the process of evolution can go in the time available to it. He points out that man, by selection, has produced an enormous variety of types of dog, such as Pekinese, bulldogs, and so on, in the space of only a few thousand years. Here "man" is the important factor in the environment, and it is his peculiar tastes that have produced (by selective breeding, not by "design") the freaks of nature we see preserved all around us as domestic dogs. Yet the time required to do this, on an evolutionary scale of hundreds of millions of years, is extraordinarily short. So we should not be surprised at the even greater variety of creatures that natural selection has produced on this much larger time scale. (*What Mad Pursuit: A Personal View of Scientific Discovery* [New York: Basic Books, 1988], p. 29)

Did you notice the fancy footwork "by selective breeding, not by 'design'?" What is selective breeding if not design? Intentional, deliberate, selective breeding is not a natural force. Animal breeders are intelligent, purposeful agents, not "factors in the environment."

The Moths Who Changed Their Colors

The peppered moth story is found in virtually all biology textbooks. It is presented as confirming evidence for Darwin's mechanism of natural selection in action. The classical scientific experiments on the peppered moth were conducted by British ecologist H. B. D. Kettlewell in the 1950s. Students and teachers should be warned, however, of several problems with these experiments. Wild peppered moths rarely, if ever, rest on tree trunks. Their usual resting place is high in the canopy under branches. Other studies have shown little correlation between lichen coloration and moth coloration. Photographs showing the moths on lichen covered tree trunks were staged, generally by pinning dead moths to the trunks. For further information on this, see Jonathan Wells, "Second Thoughts About Peppered Moths," *The Scientist,* May 24, 1999, p. 13.

Despite such problems with the peppered moth example, evidence that natural selection plays an important role in explaining small-scale microevolutionary changes is substantial. Scientific observations confirm that natural selection can produce microevolutionary changes such as variations in the leg length of lizards, size variations in guppies and antibiotic resistance in bacteria.

In summary, no one doubts that Darwin's mechanism of natural selection helps explain why populations adapt to varying environmental conditions. The unresolved question is whether the mechanism responsible for microevolutionary changes such as color variation in moths and beak sizes in birds can account for macroevolutionary innovations such as the origin of moths, birds and scientific observers in the first place.

The Dynamic Duo

Darwinists like Professor Teller see an almost miraculous generative power in mutation and natural selection. Richard Dawkins's books *The Blind Watchmaker* (New York: Norton, 1987) and *Climbing Mount Improbable* (New York: Norton, 1996) are good examples of this view. Professor Questor points out, however, that DNA functions like a language or computer. Making random changes in text or software doesn't automatically produce new sentences or functional programs. In fact, it almost always generates gibberish.

The key thought to remember from this section is that you can get variation in an existing feature (microevolution) through mutation or when existing DNA gets shuffled. But it takes new, specific information (and lots of it) to build new structures and complex organs like wings and eyes (macroevolution). As developmental biologists S. Gilbert, J. Spitz and R. Raft state,

> The Modern [new-Darwinian] Synthesis is a remarkable achievement. However, starting in the 1970's, many biologists began questioning its adequacy in explaining evolution. Genetics might be adequate for explaining microevolution, but microevolutionary changes in gene frequency were not seen as able to turn a reptile into a mammal or to convert a fish into an amphibian. Microevolution looks at adaptations that concern only the survival of the fittest, not the arrival of the fittest. ("Review: Resynthesizing Evolutionary and Developmental Biology," *Developmental Biology* 173:361)

Note that (except for the ad for "Compball's Primordial Soup") the origin of the first life from organic chemicals is not mentioned in the debate between Teller and Questor, and for good reason. Currently all naturalistic chemical evolutionary theories of the origin of life face serious problems. There is no accepted theory of chemical (as opposed to biological) evolution to debate. See standard biology texts for competing hypotheses and G. C. Mills, M. Lancaster and W. L. Bradley, "Origin of Life and Evolution in Biology Textbooks: A Critique," *The American Biology Teacher* 55, no. 2 (1993).

The Clue of the Similar Shanks

Common descent is one possible explanation for similarity but not the only one. The purpose of Professor Questor's response is not to prove that different types of vertebrates cannot be descended from one another but that they may not be. Note that intelligent design in human technology produces a pattern similar to that observed in the fossil record with major innovations or themes preceding minor variations on these themes. Designers often produce a progression of similar structures or machines (witness the history of the automobile). Nevertheless, such "common descent" does not necessarily indicate an "evolutionary relationship" or provide evidence against design.

In any case, notice back in the definitions of pages 10 and 11 that Darwinism (not intelligent purpose) was distinguished from common descent. A designer might choose to work through descent to produce a new design. Recall that on page 23 our cartoonist turned a dog into an elephant via such a progression of forms. Cartoonists frequently do this in the process of animation. This is a designed process known as "morphing."

In evaluating whether common descent or common design better explains the data, students should examine lines of evidence from the fossil record, biogeography (the geographic distribution of plants and animals), comparative anatomy, comparative biochemistry and comparative embryology. Evidence from embryology currently presented in biology textbooks is undergoing revision; the original drawings of vertebrate embryos by Ernst Haeckel we now know were manipulated to overemphasize resemblance. Further, although vertebrate embryos do pass through a stage of similarity, virtually all textbooks omit the fact that earlier in their development the vertebrate embryos are dissimilar in form, a fact that makes it questionable to invoke comparative embryology as evidence for common descent. For further information, see Jonathan Wells, "Haeckel's Embryos and Evolution: Setting the Record Straight," *The American Biology Teacher* 61, no. 25 (1999).

Toward the end of this chapter, Teller accuses Questor of "trying to sneak God into the discussion." Although Questor rightly objects to this, Teller is not alone in his accusation. A key strategy in preserving the Darwinist educational monopoly is to characterize its critics as religious fanatics trying to substitute Genesis for science, following the propaganda model of the popular play and movie *Inherit the Wind.* Design theory does not derive from religious authority of appeals to Scripture. It is a scientific inference derived from biological evidence. Calling it religion is a diversionary trick known as name-calling and is designed to prevent reasoned debate. The trick works like this: (1) misconstrue the design theory position, (2) give the misconstrued position an erroneous and derogatory label, (3) attack the label, (4) dismiss the argument.

Is the Panda's Thumb a Dumb Design?

Someone has characterized science as "a vigorous attempt to make true statements about the physical world." While many scientific inquiries begin with speculations like *Why does . . .* and *I wonder what would happen if . . . ,* we need to be very clear on the differences between testable hypotheses and simple speculation. In this story, scientific questions might include "Can the proposed Darwinian mechanism produce this observed result?" and "Is this what actually happened?" However, as Professor Questor notes, evaluating the presence (or absence) of design by guessing at the designer's purpose is more a theological or psychological question than a scientific one. The proper scientific focus is not on the supposed mental state of the supposed designer but on whether it is possible to detect design at all.

For more detail on Stephen Jay Gould's argument (and more claimed "dumb designs"), see his book *The Panda's Thumb* (New York: Norton, 1980).

With regard to Professor Teller's objection "But Darwinism is still the best naturalistic theory we have," does this mean that if the evidence is running counter to the existing materialistic paradigm, it still must stand until a new one supersedes it? When the assumption that there *will* be a naturalistic explanation becomes a philosophical commitment that there *must* be one, we have left empirical science and entered the realm of ideology.

For a more detailed discussion from the perspective of intelligent design, see William Dembski, *Intelligent Design* (Downers Grove, Ill.: InterVarsity Press, 1999).

The Case of the Missing Fossils

Punctuated equilibria was originally proposed by Stephen Jay Gould and Niles Eldridge as a model to describe the fossil record more accurately. As Gould and Eldridge noted, the fossil record shows a pattern of sudden appearance (punctuation) and stasis (equilibria or stability for long periods of time) rather than the gradual change predicted by the Darwinian mechanism.

Though punctuated equilibria describes the fossil record more accurately than Darwinism, most evolutionary biologists agree that punctuated equilibria has failed to provide a mechanism capable of producing major morphological change. Thus most biologists regard punctuated equilibria as a description, not an explanation of the pattern found in the fossil record. Darwinists attempt to reconcile their model with this more accurate description by claiming that their mechanism of gradual change does take place as Darwin predicted, but only in isolated environments or locations (such as an offshore island) that do not favor fossilization. They envision major morphological transformation occurring in these isolated locales. Once these changes have occurred, the new and improved organisms invade the more favored depositional environment (such as the mainland), thus allowing new fossil forms to "suddenly" appear. Critics wonder why

Darwinian evolution always seems to be taking place in locations that keep it from appearing in the fossil record.

The museum exhibit on page 88 is a diagrammatic representation of the "Hard Facts Wall" display at the California Academy of Sciences in Golden Gate Park in San Francisco entitled "Life Through Time: The Evidence for Evolution." The exhibit opened in 1990 and was still present as of June 1999. A classroom critical thinking exercise examining the misrepresentations in this display is contained in the book *Teaching Science in a Climate of Controversy,* available from the American Scientific Affiliation (ASA). The book can be ordered by e-mailing the ASA at <asa3@asa3.org>. It teaches students to distinguish evidence from inference and to learn to plot data independently of preconceived theories. An important lesson from this exercise is that in science it is not authority but evidence that counts.

The Biological Big Bang

"The Cambrian explosion" is the descriptive name used for the sudden appearance in the fossil record of virtually all of the animal phyla between 530 and 525 million years ago, during the Cambrian period. *Phyla* is the highest biological category of the animal kingdom, with each phylum being characterized by unique architecture—a distinct body plan or blueprint. Familiar examples of some basic animal body plans that appeared in the Cambrian explosion are cnidarians (corals and jellyfish), mollusks (clams and snails), arthropods (insects), echinoderms (starfish) and chordates (to which the vertebrates belong).

With very few exceptions, high school biology textbooks contain no information on the Cambrian explosion. No current basal text discusses the problem that this evidence presents for the Darwinian view. For additional information, see "Appendix II: The Unsolved Problem of the Cambrian Explosion" in the video study guide to the "Darwinism: Science or Naturalistic Philosophy?" debate between William Provine and Philip E. Johnson at Stanford University (available from Access Research Network by e-mail: <arn@arn.org>). See also *Time*'s cover story "Evolution's Big Bang," December 4, 1995.

Inference to the Best Explanation

The various chapters in J. P. Moreland, ed., *The Creation Hypothesis* (Downers Grove, Ill.: InterVarsity Press, 1994) and William Dembski, *Intelligent Design* (Downers Grove, Ill.: InterVarsity Press, 1999) deal with evidence of intelligent design in nature and what to make of it. For a technical discussion of the evidence for design in the information contained in DNA see Stephen C. Meyer, "DNA by Design: An Inference to the Best Explanation for the Origin of Biological Information," *Rhetoric & Public Affairs* 1, no. 4 (1998).

Richard Dawkins (p. 113) is quoted from his book *River Out of Eden* (New York: Basic Books, 1995), p. 11.

More detail on the rotary motor is given by Michael Behe in his Darwin's Black Box (New York: Free Press, 1996). A much more technical discussion of DNA as an information carrier is given by Hubert Yockey in his book *Information Theory and Molecular Biology* (Cambridge: Cambridge University Press, 1998). The mathematical and philosophical questions of distinguishing intelligent design from randomness on the one hand and law-driven natural processes on the other is detailed in William Dembski's *The Design Inference* (Cambridge: Cambridge University Press, 1998).

The Case of the Usual Suspects

Who do you think did it? How can "knowing the butler did it" interfere with a careful examination of the evidence? How might this apply to all the participants in the design versus Darwinism controversy? How might defining *science* as "seeking the best naturalistic explanation" of a phenomenon conflict with *science* as "seeking to find out what really happened"?

The elephant-as-possible suspect idea was originally suggested by a Gary Larson *Far Side* cartoon. It has also been delightfully developed by Michael Behe in his thought-provoking book *Darwin's Black Box* (p. 192):

> Imagine a room in which a body lies crushed, flat as a pancake. A dozen detectives crawl around, examining the floor with magnifying glasses for any clue to the identity of the perpetrator. In the middle of the room, next to the

body, stands a large, gray elephant. The detectives carefully avoid bumping into the pachyderm's legs as they crawl and never even glance at it. Over time the detectives get frustrated with their lack of progress but resolutely press on, looking even more closely at the floor. You see, textbooks say detectives must "get their man," so they never consider elephants.

In the study of biology, materialist detectives have "gotten their man" many times in the past. Based on this past success they insist that there must be an elephant-free solution to the mystery of life's origin too. We insist it is high time the detectives acknowledge the elephant and recognize the possibility that biological life is what it appears to be: the product of intelligent activity.

What if Darwin was wrong? What if mutation and natural selection do not have the creative power he ascribed to them? Would science come to an end? Absolutely not! But it might start having to ask some new questions.

Resources

Both Sides

An excellent presentation of both sides of the intelligent design versus Darwinism issue can be found in the video of the lively debate "Darwinism: Science or Philosophy" at Stanford University between professors Phillip Johnson (UC-Berkeley) and William Provine (Cornell). Ideal for classroom use, the video study kit contains background information, discussion questions and overheads. The kit also contains documentation of the treatment of origins in high school textbooks (produced by Access Research Network, P.O. Box 38069, Colorado Springs, CO 80937-8069; available at <www.arn.org>).

Darwinism

The most scholarly presentation of the case for Darwinism as well as for common descent can be found in Francisco J. Ayala's article "Darwin's Revolution" in *Creative Evolution!?* ed. J. H. Campbell and J. W. Schopf (Boston: Jones & Bartlett, 1994). More popular presentations can be found in books such as Oxford professor Richard Dawkins's *The Blind Watchmaker* (New York: W. W. Norton, 1987) and *Climbing Mount Improbable* (New York: W. W. Norton, 1996).

Almost all high school biology textbooks make the case for *evolution,* which sometimes means minor variation, sometimes common ancestry and sometimes simply adaptation to the environment, all of which are in some sense compatible with intelligent design. *Darwinism* is seldom spelled out explicitly.

A reader-friendly critique of Darwinism is presented in Phillip E. Johnson, *Darwin on Trial* (Downers Grove, Ill.: InterVarsity Press, 1993). The Darwinist response to intelligent design is presented in Robert T. Pennock, *Tower of Babel* (Cambridge, Mass.: MIT Press, 1999).

Intelligent Design

A good introduction to the evidence for and detection of intelligent design may be found in William A. Dembski, *Intelligent Design: The Bridge*

Between Science and Theology (Downers Grove, Ill.: InterVarsity Press, 1999). A basic overview of how to apply critical thinking to the intelligent design versus Darwinism debate is contained in Phillip E. Johnson's easy-to-understand guide *Defeating Darwinism by Opening Minds* (Downers Grove, Ill.: InterVarsity Press, 1997). A supplemental textbook for tenth-grade biology students is Percival Davis and Dean H. Kenyon, *Of Pandas and People* (Dallas: Haughton, 1993).

Michael J. Behe's *Darwin's Black Box: The Biochemical Challenge to Evolution* (New York: Free Press, 1996) is an easily understood introduction to the chemistry of life and the fascinating world of DNA. It presents the "irreducible complexity" of molecular systems (analogous to all the necessary parts to a mousetrap) as evidence against the Darwinian explanatory mechanism and evidence for intelligent design.

Most of the books listed as well as additional resources and articles may be found at <www.arn.org> or <www.discovery.org/crsc/index.html>.

For Classroom Use

A helpful resource for teachers dealing with the controversy in the classroom is *Teaching Science in a Climate of Controversy: A View from the American Scientific Affiliation,* available by e-mail at <asa3@asa3.org>. In addition to containing unanswered questions and unsolved problems not found in biology textbooks, it contains a classroom exercise in critical thinking that helps students plot data scientifically and distinguish between evidence and inference. *Science and Creationism: A View from the National Academy of Sciences* (Washington, D.C.: National Academy Press, 1999) contains a summary of the evidence for biological evolution (defined as descent with modification) although the book is inaccurate in its labeling of intelligent design theory (see background information, pp. 135-36). A scholarly treatment of intelligent design, Darwinism and the philosophy of public education is presented in *Rhetoric & Public Affairs* 1, no. 4 (1998), a special issue on the intelligent design argument, with guest editor John Angus Campbell. Single issues may be obtained from the Discovery Institute at <www.discovery.org/crsc/index.html>; phone 206-292-0401.